AT LOW TIDE

Voices of Sandy Island

athenaeum
PRESS
AT COASTAL CAROLINA UNIVERSITY
theathenaeumpress.com

The Athenaeum Press at Coastal Carolina University
Edwards College of Humanities and Fine Arts
P.O. Box 261954
Conway, South Carolina 29528-6054

Printed in the United States of America.

The Athenaeum Press is a student-centered laboratory for design, editing, publishing, and new media development. Located in the Thomas W. & Robin W. Edwards College of Humanities & Fine Arts at Coastal Carolina University in Conway, South Carolina, the press uses each publication project as a platform for enhancing undergraduate and graduate student skills across the humanities and fine arts.

TABLE OF CONTENTS

FOREWORD

On an early Saturday morning in May 2015, five Coastal Carolina University faculty and students joined me at the Sandy Island landing to meet Captain Rommy Pyatt, our tour guide. The reason for our trip was to gain a better understanding of this island's historic place within the larger Gullah Geechee community. We hoped to tell its story as a future project for the university's student-driven publishing lab, the Athenaeum Press. Pyatt arrived in a roomy pontoon boat and quickly demonstrated a natural charm and enthusiasm that eased any concerns for those of us (mostly myself) who were skittish about riding in a boat. During our two-hour tour of the island, he showed us his mother's store, school, church, and many of the homes on the island, cleverly mixing jokes, superstitions, and insightful history along the way. Although the entire trip was enjoyable, I remember mostly walking on the ever-present sand that defines the island and seeing the home of the oldest resident, 101-year-old Onethia Elliott. I just had to return to meet this woman, the great-great-granddaughter of founder Phillip Washington and the culture bearer for the island.

Sandy Island stands as a testament to Washington and other former slaves from the rice plantations on the island. After emancipation, they took fate into their own hands and built a world apart from an unfriendly white-controlled county. Throughout its history, the island had two churches, a school, four midwives, a store, and a fire department. By creating a self-reliant, cooperative community, the islanders avoided most of the "second class citizenship" experienced by African Americans during much of the twentieth century. Sandy Islanders most assuredly faced segregated bus rides to work and "Colored only" public places during trips to the mainland. However, as they traveled back across the Waccamaw River and reached their island home, they no longer had to acquiesce to white rule. It was a promised land, of sorts, a refuge that allowed Washington to found a community beholden only to itself, in the words of Langston Hughes, "on the rich soil of the world, on the rivers of the world."

From the inception of the community, Washington, who was the first pastor of New Bethel Missionary Baptist Church, along with a board of deacons, emphasized moral character and civic responsibility for everyone on the island. Over the years, residents were expected to obey God's laws first and to strive to be good citizens. Deacon Minrus Tucker stated, "All a parent can ask for is to raise good citizens." Yvonne Harris, the granddaughter he raised, became a Colonel in the U.S. Army. In fact, military service on the island traces back to the Civil War period, when Adele

Petigru Allston, widow of former South Carolina Governor Robert Allston, asked her son Benjamin about the Sandy Island slaves who ran away to join the Union Army:

"Have the young men who went into the army returned? There were a large number; July, Walker's son, Gabriel, son-in-law to Bouie and Minda, Dave, Alfred's son, and a great many others."[1]

July (Herriott), Gabriel, Dave and many others began a legacy of military service that has seen men and women from the island serve in every major war.[2] And in some instances, they gave the ultimate sacrifice. Martha Cousey recounts the final months of the life of her brother, John Henry Lance, who died in the Vietnam War. John sent her a letter in October 1967, which included the prophetic statement, "I'll be home soon, one way or another." John died on the 27th of that month, just two months before he was to return to the island.

Over the years, there was little need for a police presence on the island. Noted Southern scholar Charles Joyner described Sandy Island as a "black republic" that had its own law.[3] In 1973, a *Sun News* article found that no police officer had ever set foot on Sandy Island, and no resident could recall a crime ever being committed on the island. In the rare case of an offence or dispute, New Bethel's board of deacons took charge of the matter and resolved the issue. I encountered similar self-policing on Saint Helena Island, SC, where praise house leaders took most of the civic matters into their own hands.[4] Yet the local sheriff's department was still very visible and made arrests, especially during the Prohibition era. Obviously, the imposing Waccamaw River and Sandy Island's strong leadership kept white authorities away.

When they had to interact with the outside world, Sandy Island's leaders demonstrated an extraordinary gift for diplomacy, which enabled them to effectively petition former South Carolina governors Robert Allston and James Byrnes, and Northern philanthropist Archer Huntington. In 1859, Phillip Washington convinced Robert Allston to accept the unsound business investment of buying Sandy Island's Pipe Down Plantation and its slaves. Allston's decision, based on his deep respect for Washington, temporarily kept the slaves' families together, but it overextended his slave holdings and rendered his estate insolvent by the end of the Civil War. In the early 1930s, the island's new leader was Rev. Abraham Herriott, who convinced Archer Huntington, founder of Brookgreen Gardens, to pay for the construction of a new school on the island. Instead of an abbreviated five-month session, children now attended school for a full term, and Huntington paid for the salaries of two teachers. Huntington's admiration for Herriott is evident in the many photographs of him in the Archer and Anna Huntington archives held at Brookgreen Gardens.

Thirty years later Prince Washington, Phillip's great-great-grandson and the island's leader, successfully petitioned former Governor Byrnes to bring electricity to the community. At the news conference held shortly after he threw the switch and brought power to Sandy

Island, one state news reporter admiringly described Washington's "great dignity and poise," which rivaled the most skillful politicians in Columbia. More recently, spokesman Rev. George Weathers passionately defended the community against rich white developers, who wanted to build resort communities on the island and a bridge that was virtually off limits to Sandy Island residents. In 1996, this highly-publicized battle reached all the way to the state's capitol, prompting then-governor Beasley to encourage a compromise. The island's land is now protected as a wildlife preserve by The Nature Conservancy of South Carolina.

In times of greatest need, these leaders or "mayors" as they are often called, demonstrated an uncommon ability to guide not only their own people but powerful white men to do the right and just thing. Prince Washington used the expression the "cooperation of the common good" to describe the importance he placed on seeking a path mutually beneficial to all. Booker T. Washington expressed a similar sentiment when he offered his vision of a New South, "where mutual faith and cooperation could replace both sectional and racial hatreds."[5] Sandy Island's leaders overcame racial biases and barriers to earn respect and most importantly survival for their community.

Many people refer to Sandy Island as a Gullah Geechee community. After all, it falls squarely within the federally-designated Gullah Geechee Cultural Heritage Corridor, which extends along the coast from Wilmington, North Carolina to Jacksonville, Florida. Moreover, this island community's geographic isolation and unquestionable connections to West African agricultural techniques, religious practices, language, musical traditions, and rice-based cuisine are defining characteristics of Gullah Geechee culture. This island's rich history, however, reveals a community defiant in the face of slavery, Jim Crowism, a lack of basic utilities, rich white land developers, and even the broad labeling of Gullah Geechee. Today's residents recount their ancestors' lessons and values that are a source of pride and understanding of their island's unique importance in South Carolina history. Joyner explains, "My sense is that pride and ancestry is a bit stronger [here] than in most places."[6]

Our time spent on Sandy Island has taught faculty members and students to focus less on this community's connections to other islands such as Johns, Edisto, Daufuskie, and St. Helena and more on the individual stories of the Herriott, Pyatt, Elliott, Deas, Tucker, Weathers, Allston, Collins, Lance, Robinson, Youngs, Simmons and Washington families. We found our greatest triumphs when we simply helped to carry a refrigerator from Charles Pyatt's boat into his home or conducted genealogy sessions during Saturday computer sessions with the seniors in the community. In these informal interactions, residents graciously shared invaluable information about their own history. By celebrating the importance of their individuality, their family, we better understood how these threads of life fit upon the Sandy Island's story quilt. The national recognition of the Gullah Geechee culture has brought much-needed funding and increased awareness of the unifying elements found in many of the African American island communities. Yet it is equally important to recognize the individual differences in each community's history and their unique contributions to the whole of the African American experience in the South.

A few weeks after my initial trip to the island, I met Mrs. Onethia, as she is fondly called, in her home. After giving me a warm greeting, she began to interview me for a few minutes and ask where I was from. After explaining my Virginia roots and my interest in Sandy Island's history, she openly discussed her memories of Sandy Island and her wonderful life on the island. I was amazed by her quick wit, genuine interest in my life, and her sharpness of thought—Barack Obama was her President! In each successive interview with Mrs. Onethia, I learned something new about the island's history and the remarkable ability of this community to persevere in the face of tragedy. Each of the remaining residents on the island has lost at least one loved one to drowning. Over the years, the Waccamaw River served as a natural barrier between Sandy Island and the Jim Crow south on the mainland, but it came at the price of over twenty drowning deaths.

Although I believed I understood the strength of this community, Mrs. Onethia again taught me about strength two years later upon the tragic death of her great-granddaughter, Jamisa Lewis. Jamisa's funeral was held in the gymnasium of her high school on Saturday, March 11, 2017. As I arrived at the school, I thought it unlikely that I would see Mrs. Onethia. How could someone more than 100 years old manage the strength to catch a car to the boat landing, ride a boat over to the mainland, walk to the car, and then endure a long funeral procession? But as the family slowly entered, I saw this woman, with the aid of a walker, will her body to walk from the back of the gym to the front, so she could see her great-grandchild one last time. This great-great-granddaughter of Phillip Washington refused to give in to tragedy, physical limitations, and even, perhaps, her own mortality. It was as if she were saying, "I am still here, and I am going to walk to see Jamisa." At that moment, she called upon the strength of those ancestors who came before her.

Sandy Island's current spokesmen, Rev. George Weathers and Charles Pyatt, follow in the footsteps of Phillip Washington, Abraham Herriott, and Prince Washington, who established the principles of good will and cooperation, which has sustained the island for over a century. Equally important are Laura Herriott, Celia Pyatt, Theresa Weathers, Beulah Pyatt, Sara Deas and Angelis Washington, who stand on the shoulders of pioneering female educational and religious leaders such as Louise Tucker, Emily Collins Pyatt, and Rebecca Washington. However, where there were once hundreds of African American residents on the island, less than forty remain—the footsteps are becoming fewer and far between.

Low Tide: Voices of Sandy Island offers a unique exploration of this African American community's rich history and sheer will to survive despite nearly insurmountable odds. This project is based on extensive historical research and fieldwork conducted over a two-year period. With the assistance of Coastal Carolina University students Quinten Ameris and Brooks Leibee, I interviewed many of the island's residents and family members living in neighboring cities. During these wonderful encounters, we let them tell their own story in their own way. Shonte Clement, Jesse Linder, Maggie Nichols, Ronda Taylor, and Madia Walker helped bring this history to life. I believe you will discover, as we did, the treasure that is Sandy Island.

ERIC CRAWFORD
Assistant Professor of Music, Coastal Carolina University

---

[1] Robert Allston and J. H. Easterby, *The South Carolina Rice Plantation As Revealed in the Papers of Robert F.W. Allston*, (Columbia, S.C.: University of South Carolina Press, 2004), 223.

[2] J. Raymond Gourdin, *Borrowed Identity: 128th United States Colored Troops: Multiple-Name Usage by Black Civil War Veterans Who Served with Union Regiments Organized in South Carolina* (Westminster, MD: Heritage Books, 2009).

[3] Christopher Kouri, "When a Man Starts Out to Build a World: The History of Sandy Island," Penn Center Sea Island Preservation Project, (St. Helena Island, South Carolina, 1994). 43.

[4] Praise houses were small structures on each plantation, where slaves met for evening prayer services. All civic matters were decided also in these one-room dwellings. See Patricia Guthrie, *Catching Sense: African American Communities on a South Carolina Sea Island* (Westport Conn: Bergin & Garvey, 1996). Guthrie discusses the continued survival of praise houses on St. Helena Island long after they disappeared on other surrounding islands.

[5] Booker T. Washington, "Atlanta Compromise Speech," (Cotton States and International Exposition, Atlanta, 18 September 1895).

[6] Cited in Kouri, 6-7. See also Charles Joyner, *Down by the Riverside: A South Carolina Slave Community*, (Urbana: University of Illinois Press, 2009), 7-8.

HEALTH ADVISORY
ADVERTENCIA SOBRE LA SALUD
WACCAMAW RIVER

TOURS
de
SANDY
ISLAND
TOUR TIMES
& PRICES
WWW.ToursdeSandyIsland.com
843 408 7187

THE CROSSING

A pontoon sets out from the mainland carrying its passengers the short distance to Sandy Island. Trees line the riverbanks, a slight chill hanging in the air as a heavy fog hangs just above the trees. There is little wind; the Waccamaw is calm. Suddenly, the pontoon clears the corridor of trees to reveal the river's main channel and the next stop comes into view. The landing at Sandy Island seems so close, its shoreline calling the boat home.

Sandy Island housed nine plantations in the nineteenth century: Oak Hampton, Ruinville, Brickville, Mount Arena, Sandy Knowe, Oak Lawn, Holly Hill, Pipe Down, and Hassell Hill. Today's African American community easily traces many of its ancestors to Pipe Down and Mount Arena. After the Civil War ended and the Thirteenth Amendment abolished slavery, freed slaves on the island bought the land they had worked their entire lives, founding a community of their own. While the river shielded the islanders from the outside world, it provided its own unique challenges as well. There was no easy access to goods and services on the mainland because there was no bridge to the island, and the unpredictable current of the Waccamaw often made it

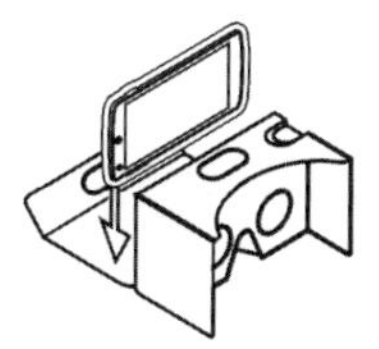

Experience the crossing to Sandy Island by visiting ccu.press/vr.

impossible to determine if the river was passable from the shore. However, it was the only option the islanders had.

Beginning in the 18th century, the Waccamaw River served as a major trade route for white landowners who sent their indigo, cotton, and rice crops up and down the river, linking the county seats of Horry and Georgetown. Even earlier, Eastern Sioux tribes traveled and hunted on the river and named it "Waccamaw," which means coming and going, because of its two-daily tides. Connecting the Lowcountry to Chesapeake Bay in Virginia, the river became part of the Intracoastal Waterway in the 1930s, helping to move bulk materials efficiently along the Atlantic Seaboard. During this time, U.S. Route 17 was built through the Waccamaw Neck, and the orientation of the community shifted further to the shore and the developing outside world.

Photo of the Georgetown *Comanche*, which traveled up and down the Waccamaw River. Image courtesy of the Pawleys Island Civic Association.

The Waccamaw River provided an abundance of sturgeon, mullet, garfish, brim, bass, trout, catfish, and especially shad fish for the island's population. For most of the twentieth century, shad fishermen on the island sold their large hauls to local merchants, including men such as Herman Gordon, the owner of a local fish market and ice house, who traveled to the island to buy fish. The shad fishing season lasted from January until Easter, providing money and food for the islanders' families. The fishermen were highly skilled at predicting where the fish were most abundant, the safest time to navigate the river, or whether to go out onto the river at all.

Fishnets and Boats on Sandy Island, circa 1930s. Image courtesy of Brookgreen Gardens.

When the Sandy Island community was first established, residents traveled in row boats to a landing connected to Brookgreen Plantation located at present-day Brookgreen Gardens, approximately three miles away. Until the late

ONETHIA ELLIOTT

"Sandy Island is my home. I was born and raised here. No place I'd rather be than on Sandy Island."

1950s, residents had no motorized boats—the only option was to pick up the oars and row. Franklin Tucker, who was born and raised on the island, remembered the journey taking as long as an hour, depending on the tide, and there were often many trips made in the course of a day. A closer landing and motorized boats has shortened the journey, cutting the time from an hour to under ten minutes. But the very act of crossing remains dangerous.

February 18, 2009: a storm is coming. Six islanders push their boat away from the mainland, hoping to make it across before the weather turns. The water is choppy, and the wind bites into the sides of the shallow hull. The landing is only 30 yards away; the motor working as hard as it is able. A gust capsizes the boat. All six passengers fall into the water. Tiffany Tucker, the boat's operator, pulls herself and her daughter onto the shore and calls to the Pyatt family, who live closest to shore. Charles Pyatt pushes his small boat out into the water, and pulls out Zyair Smalls, a nine-month-old boy, floating near the boat's wrecked seats in what he later describes as a cradle of clothes. For twenty-seven hours, boats from on and off the island search the waters. Shaquatia Robinson is pulled from the water, but passes at the hospital. Her mother, Lou Ann, and Rishard Pyatt, perish in the waters.

Willis Robinson, the brother and uncle of the Robinsons, describe the event as a nightmare that must be overcome. Even after a year, one Georgetown resident involved in the search for survivors still remembers the tragic event clearly. However, loss is met with perseverance. Sandy

Islander Herman Elliott simply states, "Time must go on." According to Rosalind Geathers, Zyair's maternal grandmother, the love the people of Sandy Island have for one another knits the community together in times of tragedy. The force of the Waccamaw is met with the force of the island.

In the words of Angelis Pyatt Washington, "Be careful when the Waccamaw is angry." Drownings that occurred from the mid 1950s to 2009 remind the islanders to always watch the tides carefully, trying to gauge what the river will do the next day or even hour. The water often seems uncaring about the lives it takes. The shore is too close to be so far.

But today, the water is calm, the journey short. The wind passing over the dock barely hints at colder weather to come. It is easy to think the ride always feels this easy. But sometimes the wind howls and bites into the passenger's skin. The water is not always calm, and at these times it is best to leave the river alone.

When approaching Sandy Island, the Pyatt General Store serves as a bright beacon from across the Waccamaw.

Just beyond the landing, the soft white sand peppered with grass invites the passengers home. The tide gently laps at the shore. The oaks offer centuries of reassurance. The general store owned by Samuel and Beulah Pyatt serves as a beacon with its cheery yellow paint and red roof. Houses built by the islanders stand to greet visitors with their welcoming structures. Grounded in history and pride, Sandy Island is home to a people who have been there for centuries. Their ancestors landed at the same landing, walked the same sandy roads, built and rebuilt houses, an entire community—a refuge across the river. This is home, comfortable, slow, hand built brick by brick.

FOUNDING AN ISLAND

Wind gusts cross the riverfront, pass the yellow walls of Pyatt's General Store, and travel up the hill through oak trees that shuffle their strong gray branches in the wind. The air swoops down into the lowland over sandy paths where oxen once roamed. At Windover Road, the wind rustles the leaves that lay amid the grave markers of forefathers and former slaves. The breeze moves onward, wafting about Mount Arena's sandy knolls, brushing gently across the homesteads of Weathers, Elliotts, Robinsons, Tuckers, Pyatts, and Herriotts. Just ahead stands a beacon.

New Bethel Baptist Church today. This church building, built in 1951, sits yards away from the original church foundation, raised in 1880.

The white steeple with a cross at its crest glows in the sun. Aquamarine stained windows sparkle under the beaming sun, and fresh white paint gives the building a fresh vitality. New Bethel Missionary Baptist Church, originally built by Sandy Islanders in 1880, has served as the church home for generations of families who worked to ensure a better future for themselves after freedom. The foundation of the original church sits just a stone's throw from the church's newly-remodeled entrance. Sandy Island resident Charles Pyatt along with men from the church constructed a new bathroom and stairs leading into the sanctuary's vestibule.

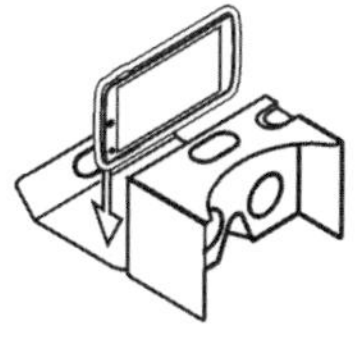

See a church service at New Bethel by visiting ccu.press/vr.

As in the past, the skilled tradesmen on Sandy Island take pride in the appearance of New Bethel.

Out in the churchyard, gravestones mark the lineage of those who etched their stories into the island's legacy. Some are mothers and daughters, others are soldiers and sons, and some are victims of the Waccamaw River. In the back center lies siblings Shelia, Bentlee, Eva and their cousin James Herriot, who drowned in Thoroughfare Creek on June 19, 1973. These children died while trying to rescue one who had fallen off a wooden board and into the water. They lie next to their ancestors, next to generations after them. Each body that rests in the graveyard is a part of the island's long history.

Before the Civil War, Georgetown County's rice export created some of the richest men in America. Yet the dozens of rice plantations along the Waccamaw Neck and Sandy Island were built on the backs of West African slaves. It was the slaves who knew when to flood the fields, clear the cypress wetlands, and how to dig the rice canals. Alongside this expertise, these slaves brought with them unique threads of cultures that were woven through generations. Sandy Island's families trace their ancestry to this slavery period, when their ancestors worked the land for a white master.

Captain Thomas and Mary Anne Petigru owned Pipe Down Plantation on Sandy Island. As a naval officer, Petigru used the nautical term "pipe down" to describe the quiet and peacefulness on the island, and the Petigrus were one of the few white families who lived on the island with their slaves, instead of on the mainland. They were also related by blood or marriage to the most notable families in Georgetown, including the LaBruce and Allston families. Mrs. Petigru, sister-in-law of South Carolina Governor Robert Allston, brought her own personal wealth into the marriage.

Counter-clockwise, from top left: Image of boat tied to shore, historic Sandy Island home, Abraham Herriott fanning rice on Sandy Island, island resident thrashing rice after harvest, landing on Sandy Island at dusk. Historic images courtesy of Brookgreen Gardens.

Thomas Petigru earned a reputation as a philanderer and alcoholic, but he was known to treat his slaves reasonably well. In 1857, Captain Petigru, for some the only master they had ever known, died suddenly. With his passing, Mary Anne Petigru wanted to move elsewhere and sell the plantation, including its assets, the people enslaved on Pipe Down. These slaves knew they had to stop the auctions of their family and friends to the highest bidder. If not, families would be broken apart, some would be forced to leave Sandy Island forever.

The community took it upon themselves to find a new master of their plantation. Few among them had the experience needed to broker a deal with any white landowner. However, the slave driver on Pipe Down, the leader among the slaves who motivated the people to work through the long days and interacted with the white master, took up the task. Phillip Washington, a man described by

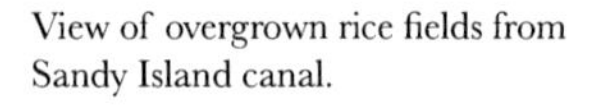
View of overgrown rice fields from Sandy Island canal.

Elizabeth Allston Pringle as "a very tall, very black man, a splendid specimen of the Negro race," set out to save the island community.

Captain Petigru admired Washington's intelligence and wit, and dictated in his will that he be freed upon his death. But emancipation was illegal in South Carolina, so Washington continued in his role as the slaves' driver. He was still a slave, but he had the power of persuasion.

Washington set his sights on Mrs. Petigru's brother-in-law, Governor Allston, to buy Pipe Down. Alston was considered a fair master who already owned much of the land along the Waccamaw. Washington had to make multiple visits, but Allston agreed to purchase Petigru's slaves in 1859, despite owning an overabundance of both land and slaves. Washington's triumph would be short lived, however. Within two years, South Carolina seceded from the United States and the Civil War erupted. As white owners left their homes to support the war efforts, plantations were seized, and many slaves left the plantations to join the Union.

In 1864, Governor Allston died, and after the end of the war Congress granted full citizenship to freed men and women of color, changing forever the rice industry centered in the Waccamaw Neck. Free to seize new opportunities, Washington and a few other residents left the island. Washington became a successful businessman with a home on Georgetown's prosperous Front Street. The post-war Reconstruction period initially bolstered the fortunes of many African Americans in Georgetown County, who

WINDOVER DR
STOP
NO PARKING

controlled a majority of the county's seats in the Legislature and control over public education.

Although the remaining islanders decided to continue rice cultivation on the island, much like before, they did not own the land on which they lived and worked. The federal promise of forty acres and a mule was not kept. Instead, Former Confederate landowners, whose plantations had been seized by the federal government, reacquired their old plantations—the freed men and women on Sandy Island were still in servitude.

When federal occupation ended in 1877, White backlash followed the removal of the troops, and African Americans experienced overt racism and few economic opportunities in the city. By 1878, Washington responded to this changing climate by returning to the Waccamaw and Sandy Island to build a sanctuary on his island home.

Washington purchased land on Sandy Island from Mrs. Petigru to build a church the community named New Bethel Baptist Church. Two years later, he purchased nearly 300 acres of the Mount Arena property for his family and friends. Another resident, James Pyatt, made two land purchases totaling 634 acres of land. At the time of Washington's death in December of 1890, at the age of 83, his estate was valued at $5,900, roughly equivalent to $150,000 in today's market. He had further secured bank bonds totaling another $16,000 in today's dollars. Washington distributed this wealth among his family members, who continued his legacy of community leadership..

Phillip Washington's Georgetown residence on Front Street.

Washington and the other founding members created a self-directed community that understood the importance of owning land, which was a status unavailable to most African Americans. These former slaves passed their invaluable rice-growing skills and traditions on to their children, who were born free. In turn, the history of rice cultivation on Sandy Island continued well into the 20th century as the islanders grew rice to feed themselves and their families.

The Nature Conservancy of South Carolina now owns much of the land on Sandy Island and protects the wildlife on the island. To this day, however, foundations of the old slave cabins remain among the brush and stand as testaments of the beginning of a community whose history and legacy continues.

CAROLINA GOLD

Before the sun rises and the other slaves on the plantation wake up, a tall, dark-skinned man prepares himself for the coming day. It is his job to ensure that all the workers in the slave quarters set off to the fields on time and know their tasks for the day. The slave driver situates his high boots, fine shirt, and blue jacket. Phillip Washington is well respected by all those on the plantation. His new master, Robert Allston, respects him more than any other worker on the plantation. The slaves trust him to see them through the arduous tasks and trials of the day. As his day begins, the coolness of the early morning will soon be a distant memory in the heat of the coming June day.

Washington looks out over the broad rice fields that have been flooded in the spring to sprout the rice crop. Washington hopes he was correct in promising Allston a good crop, "if the weather holds, and we avoid storms." To make sure, he is attempting a full flooding method on two-thirds of the fields to protect the heavy stalks. This is the second flooding. The first was to let the sprouts grow, and the third will be to fatten the rice before harvest.

A man uses oxen to plow the rice field to allow for proper irrigation. Image courtesy of Brookgreen Gardens.

Rice bales dot the landing, most likely in the Mount Arena area of Sandy Island. Image courtesy of Brookgreen Gardens.

They planted this year rice a little early, the third week of March. This flood is on schedule, here at the end of June, to harvest in the fall. Once taken from the fields, rice will be dried in barns and then threshed with two long sticks tied together with a piece of leather at the top. When the threshing is complete, slaves beat the rice with oar-like pestles, and fanned the rice in large winnowing baskets to separate the grain from the husk. A proficient worker could produce about a gallon of refined rice in just half an hour.

Although cotton was better known as the cash crop of the South, rice—or "Carolina Gold" as it was called—was the dominant crop in the Georgetown County region before the Civil War. Slaves from the rice-growing countries in West Africa were highly prized on plantations because of their extensive knowledge of the crop. They knew how much water should flood the field and how to create a hole down the center of large trunks, which would then be tightly plugged and unplugged to control the water. Later, a more sophisticated pulley system lifted and lowered a gate to control the flow of water.

During a long cultivation process, slaves had to bear the full weight of South Carolina's challenging climate and landscape. The sun seared their backs as they worked up to 10 hours at a time. Sweat from the heat soaked their clothes, while the mud from the wet fields caked their feet. Moisture in the humid air made it difficult for them to catch their breath, and the risk of heat stroke was high. Due to hot temperatures, diseases spread faster, and the wet conditions invited mosquitoes and other disease-carrying pests into the wetlands. Slaves had to also be mindful of environmental dangers such as alligators and snakes, and, because it was illegal to teach slaves to swim, drownings posed an equal danger. More than one-third of the slaves arriving from West Africa died within three years.

During the 1850s, rice cultivation was the main work done on the nine plantations housed on Sandy Island, including the plantations of Mount Arena and Pipe Down, from which most of Sandy Island's African American community is descended. With the exception of the Pipe Down worker's former owner, Captain Petigru, most planters did not live on their plantation. Instead, they chose to spend most of their time in their Georgetown city homes, leaving the driver and the overseer to manage the plantation. Though slaves worked in the field by themselves, they had to complete the tasks assigned to them by the slave driver and the overseer, or face the consequences.

Women in Georgetown pounding rice during the 1920s. Image courtesy of the Georgetown Digital Public Library.

Masters tasked drivers with disciplining the slaves and required them to carry a whip at all times. Yet there is no record of Phillip Washington ever whipping a slave, and he was regarded as the patriarch of the slave community. Trusted by Robert Allston, master of Pipe Down Plantation, and all those under him, Washington united the enslaved community on Sandy Island after the death of Captain Petigru in 1857. He successfully organized his workers to produce rice that was formally recognized for its distinct sweetness and quality—Carolina Gold won a silver medal (1855) and a gold medal (1856) at the Paris Exposition for the cultivation of rice. Another nearby planter, Dr. Thomas Heriot, won an award at the 1851 London World's Fair for his crop.

Plantation owners attempted to continue rice cultivation in the Georgetown County region through the Civil War, but a lack of slave labor and the crumbling southern economy made the industry a lost cause. Furthermore, successive hurricanes devastated the rice industry in the Georgetown region in the early 1900s. Ravaging the land, destroying crops, and leaving chaos in their wake, the hurricanes made it unprofitable to salvage the rice crop in Georgetown. This collapsing industry only made Sandy Island stronger. Under the leadership of chief foreman Abraham Herriot, residents continued to grow rice on the island long after the rest of the region ceased production.

On an afternoon in 1932, Herriot steps onto the rice field to survey the land. The rice is high, and it will be harvested

A woman and her child pause from pounding the rice, circa 1930s. Image courtesy of Brookgreen Gardens.

soon. Autumn wind glides across the field like a gentle whisper; this may be the last harvest Sandy Island will ever produce. With sturdy frame and high head, he accepts the coming end to his island's historic work with proud accomplishment. He contemplates how his island's self-reliance and connectedness matches that of his ancestors'.

CHARLES PYATT

"Growing up on the island, I figured if you need wood, you just go and get wood. I had cut down a tree, and some men came out of the woods, and they asked 'You know whose land you're on?' and I said, 'No, and I really don't care.' Because at that time, I figure on Sandy Island, you could go anywhere you want to go."

Two Sandy Island residents pounding rice, circa 1930s. Image courtesy of Brookgreen Gardens.

Two Sandy Island residents fanning rice with hulls into a pestle, circa 1930s. Image courtesy of Brookgreen Gardens.

The slaves worked in the rice fields together, and passed it down for generations to come. "Our history is here," he says, rooted as firmly as the rice in the fields he stands on.

Herriot moves to the landing to meet those coming back to help with the rice harvest. Over the past thirty years, making a living on the island has become harder. Islanders must leave to find work, and many move to the mainland where there are paved roads and no worries about crossing a river to get to work. But this is home, and the people who leave always come back to help with growing the rice. It calls them back to cherish and strengthen their identity. Sandy Island may lose residents as time goes on, but the familial bonds that hold them together will not break with distance.

Soon enough, the very last sprout of rice will be planted. Until that time, Herriott will wait at the landing for his family to come home and share in the legacy their ancestors left for them. Working with the rice may not be around for much longer, but right now bonds remain from blood and sweat left in this dirt.

Prior to the last crop in the 1940s, rice fed those on the island, and residents exchanged or sold excess rice for goods from the mainland. Rice profits bought land, bought freedom. Men, women, and children participated in the growing, harvesting, and refining the crop. Franklin Tucker remembers being old enough to refine the rice when it was brought in from the rice fields as a child growing up on the island. Onethia Elliott, a 102 year old resident, remembers dehusking the rice in waist high mortars with long pestles.

These were chores that many of the children on the island were glad to do. When asked about fanning and beating rice, daughter of Sandy Island residents, Martha Cousey simply said, "It was fun doing what we did."

The enslaved West Africans brought to the plantations in the South came from many different cultures and backgrounds, but their ability to form close, familial bonds with others helped them endure a difficult existence. Barnyards containing the valuable rice were not locked, because those on the island were confident no one would steal anything. Animals that were butchered were freely offered to anyone who asked, and the rice harvest was also shared by all on the island. The community sustained itself by caring for its own, a value continued through each generation of Sandy Islanders.

BUILDING AN ISLAND

Prior to emancipation, plantation owners often paid for a minister to come and preach to their slaves. Robert Allston even built a prayer house for his slaves and proudly stated that they were "greatly improved in intelligence and morals." However, almost immediately after gaining their freedom, the men and women of Sandy Island bought land for themselves to build their own church. Phillip Washington purchased land on the island and built New Bethel Missionary Baptist Church in 1880. The original structure, made of wood and with a balcony, became the foundation of their newly liberated community. Over the course of the next century and a half, New Bethel remained the most important institution on the island.

United, the new congregation of New Bethel possessed the power to shape and organize their community for themselves. First pastored by Phillip Washington until his death in 1890 the church's first deacon board was Ned Huger, Francis Washington (Phillip's son), Tom Keith, Andrew Rhode, and July Herriot, who succeeded Washington as pastor.

New Bethel's deacons played a crucial role in maintaining order on Sandy Island. Although the island is typically a peaceful place, there have been times when the board of deacons, a group of about six church members, had to take law enforcement into their own hands. In a *Sun News* interview with Prince Washington in 1973, Washington said, there was little use for police officers on the island: "If the offender committed an act of wrongdoing which is significant, he is taken to the church to be dealt with." By working together, islanders monitored and enforced the law upon themselves. "In most cases the treatment is effective… we puts the fear of the Almighty into him. He seldom make the same mistake twice."

During the mid-19th century, registered Black voters outnumbered white voters 861 to 814 in Georgetown County, and Sandy Island had surprising legislative power. Voting precincts setup throughout the county included large pockets of African American constituents, including the voting precinct at New Bethel Missionary Baptist Church on Sandy Island. The island community exerted voting strength because many of its residents owned their land and met the necessary land ownership requirements to become registered voters. Also, the community voted as one for the same candidate. With the island's help, African American candidates were elected to the South Carolina House of Representatives. These men were B.H. Williams, J.A. Baxter, and John Bolts.

The power to elect Black men into Congress stemmed largely from the individual voting precincts, and some of the surrounding white community wanted to eliminate Sandy Island's political influence in the Waccamaw region.

In 1886, the *Georgetown Enquirer* published an article openly soliciting multiple efforts to "knock the spots out of Sandy Island." However, these attempts were not initially successful, and in both 1898 and 1900, former Sandy Islander school teacher John Bolts was elected to the South Carolina House of Representatives. He would be the last African American in the South Carolina House of Representatives for the next seventy years. At the turn of the century, Georgetown County removed the voting precinct on Sandy Island and instituted even harsher voting requirements for African Americans.

Genevieve Chandler Peterkin, noted Southern writer and Georgetown County civil rights advocate, volunteered at the voting precinct's new location in the 1970s, and she considered the Sandy Island community to be "the most civic-minded people." Peterkin found a nearly 100% voter participation by the community despite the often cold weather journey across the river in November for the senior

WEDNESDAY MORNING, AUG. 4, 1886.

The New Constitution.

The only way in which you can help to control the next election for county officers is to sign the club rolls. No more precincts. Hereafter, for instance, Georgetown will be entitled to one delegate to every ten names on the roll. This plan knocks the spots out of Sandy Island and materially reduces the representation from Waccamaw.—*Times*.

1886 clipping of "The New Constitution" in the Georgetown Enquirer. Image from the Georgetown Digital Public Library.

adults. She observed that candidates would noticeably appeal to Prince Washington, the island's leader. His influential endorsement guaranteed the full support of the island.

Two other leaders, Deacon Prince Washington and Rev. Abraham Herriot, successfully advocated for much needed services and a schoolhouse for the community. Prince Washington, chairman of the deacon board in the 1950's and 1960's, petitioned for the installation of utilities on the island over the span of two decades. Abraham Herriot, a minister and foreman of the island's rice crops during the 1930's and 1940's, was responsible for asking philanthropist Archer Huntington to build a schoolhouse on Sandy Island. Images courtesy of Brookgreen Gardens and the Georgetown Digital Public Library.

The spiritual experience at New Bethel followed the established practices of the Baptist church with the exception of the seekin' ritual for church membership. Until the latter half of the 20th century, seekin', an abbreviation for "seeking Christ," was a journey to spiritual awakening and coming of age for a young adult. Seekin' is a Gullah Geechee tradition that represents a young person's readiness to become a member of the church. In this ritual, a teenager between the ages of 10-14 would shun all social contact and wander out into the wilderness alone at midnight until experiencing a dream or vision of a spiritual parent. This guide was usually an elderly woman or man of high esteem in the community who was well versed in the lessons of the Bible. During this time, "seekers" wore a white string or cloth around their heads as a signal to the community of their spiritual quest and girls placed ash on their faces. Seekin' was both a test of will and a test of faith in God and sometimes took several weeks for a young person to complete. Once a spiritual guide was confident that the young person, new the tenets of the Bible, the deacons of the church administered an oral exam to the candidate.

On Sandy Island, a more moderate form of seekin' developed in the twentieth century. Seekers did not have to shun the community and go out into the wilderness in order to have a vision of their spiritual guide. Young candidates simply chose their spiritual guides from the deacons and deaconesses of New Bethel Baptist. Laura Herriott was 13 when she chose Louise Tucker, a deaconess of New Bethel at the time, to be her spiritual mother. Laura remembered, "She would tell me to come to her home at 5 o'clock, and then you seek there until dark, 'cause I guess you're not gonna be afraid if you are seekin'. After she feels like I'm ready with the questions she gives me, she'll tell the pastor, 'She's ready.'" Though the practice of seekin' differed throughout the various insulated communities along the Lowcountry of South Carolina and coastal Georgia, traditions like seekin' were an important legacy from the slave experience that carried forward on Sandy Island.

Another church, Butler Chapel African Methodist Episcopal Church, was founded in 1937. The earliest known pastor of Butler Chapel was George Washington, who came from Charleston in the 1940s. His wife Stella taught school on the island and Sandy Islander Emily Collins Pyatt remembers her showing the women on the island how to make mattresses out of cotton, which were much softer than their straw mattresses. Because members of this church came from the Belin section of the island, the church faced toward this community. Butler Chapel had fewer members than New Bethel and had no choir. Former resident Arthur Herriott remembers, "the pastor usually started a song and everyone joined in." By the 1970s there were only 9-10 members, so the pastor of the church, Alex Kinlaw, asked Herriott to serve as both trustee and steward. Shortly after this period, the remaining members joined with New Bethel.

Glue-All

American
Red Cross

Clockwise, from top left. The Sandy Island School in 1969; the school house today. Island residents standing outside the school house in 1969: (left to right) Edgar Washington; Onethia Elliot; unidentified; Rosetta Pyatt; Louise Tucker; Rebecca Washington; Mary Nelson; Lucille Herriott; James Herriott, Sr. Historic images courtesy of Brookgreen Gardens.

Butler Chapel's corner stone.

Butler Chapel and New Bethel had strong family ties and a spirit of cooperation over the many years of their coexistence. For instance, New Bethel gave some of their pews to Butler Chapel for their sanctuary. Also, on the second and fourth Sundays when neither church had a pastor, both congregations came together for a joint service. In 2000, the Nature Conservancy knocked down the remaining sections of the old Butler Chapel structure, but a former member took the church's cornerstone to her home on Sandy Island, where it now sits in the front yard.

Leadership on the island has always been tied to the leadership in New Bethel. July Herriott, a former Union soldier, followed Phillip Washington as pastor of New Bethel. Other notable pastors were S.A. Green, J.R. Matthews, and Thomas Ford, who came to the island in the 1990s as the first full-time pastor for the church. Under the guidance of current pastor Karon Jackson, the church purchased two church buses and a church boat to bring members over from the mainland. Some notable deacons were R.A. Fishburn, Aaron Young, Enoch Collins, Prince Washington, Jeff Heriott, William Collins, Minrus Tucker, Arthur Washington and James Herriott who helped to organize a senior citizens group that met in the schoolhouse during the 1970s.

Children on their way to the Sandy Island school house, led by their teacher, circa 1930s. Image courtesy of Brookgreen Gardens.

Education was as valuable as faith to Sandy Islanders during the late 1800's and early 1900's. Though they had impromptu house-schools, the island's leaders realized the importance of contemporary teaching methods and resources if they wanted to keep up with the developing world. Likewise, as the south instituted Jim Crow laws and practices, it became even more important for the people of

A boy peeks out of his doorway on Sandy Island, circa 1930s. Image courtesy of Brookgreen Gardens.

Emily Collins Pyatt.

Sandy Island to have a true school building. In 1932, Rev. Abraham Herriott approached millionaire philanthropist Archer Huntington, who had just purchased land nearby, about building a schoolhouse on Sandy Island. In the spirit of Phillip Washington, Herriott's persuasion was successful.

Huntington, a wealthy northerner and husband to renowned sculptor Anna Hyatt, acquired roughly 9,100 acres that stretched from the Atlantic Ocean to the Waccamaw. He and his wife developed this land into a scenic property that houses art and other sculptures called Brookgreen Gardens. Upon Herriott's request, Huntington donated enough money to build a two-room concrete school building on the island and to pay the salaries of two teachers. "When Mr. Huntington came, he said he found an island of people," said Emily Collins Pyatt, who was born on Sandy Island and taught at the school for many years. "We quickly let him know he didn't find an island of people." Instead, the islanders found him and again ensured a future for themselves.

Leadership at the schoolhouse differed slightly from New Bethel on Sandy Island. The church was led by the pastor and the board of deacons, who were exclusively men. These men were often older and highly respected among the other islanders. With the exception of the aforementioned John Bolts, Dolan Bland (known affectionately as Prof.), and Nathaniel Herriott, most of the school's teachers were young women like Emily Pyatt, who graduated from Benedict College in Columbia, SC. In 1943, her first year

Clockwise, from top left: Children on the Mount Arena landing with their ox, the primary form of transportation on the island until the 1950s. The interior of the Sandy Island schoolhouse, now community center with books donated by Coastal Carolina University. The first school boat, the *Prince Washington*, docked on the landing at the mainland. Historic images courtesy of Brookgreen Gardens.

of teaching, some families on the island questioned Pyatt's abilities as an instructor. In her words, "Some on the island didn't think I knew enough to teach their children so they sent them to Miss Ruby Forsythe's school," which was on the mainland. Yet the islanders quickly grew to respect Pyatt's teaching methods and strict discipline, and she remembers her teaching experience as "good years." In fact, Pyatt's students who attended Howard High School often found themselves "more advanced than the other students," and many of her former students still keep in contact with her even today. Pyatt lives in Pawleys Island now but still returns to the island for the family reunions.

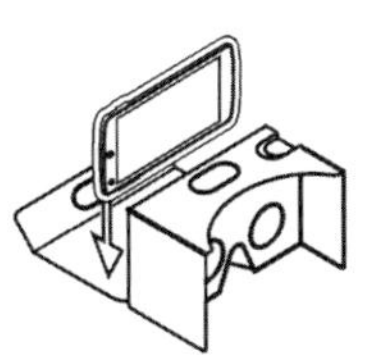

Tour the historic Sandy Island School by visiting ccu.press/vr.

The Sandy Island School served students from grades 1-7, when it was first built, and later grades 1-6. Pyatt usually taught the upper division, grades, 4-7, while another teacher taught the primary division grades 1-3. Other notable teachers were Janie Lee, Anna Nelson, Cleo Jackson, Mattie Keith and Minnie Williams. Currently in her mid 90s, Mrs. Collins Pyatt recalls a saying she learned from her father, Enoch Collins, that sustained her throughout her teaching career: "Walking slow will not keep you from getting there...try, try, again."

CROSSING BACK OVER

The Waccamaw is calm as Onethia Elliott wakes for work. She rises from her bed before the sun, muscles already aching, their minds leaning toward evening and the sounds of their children playing in the afternoon sun. Until then, the older children will look after the younger—the elder women on the island will keep an eye out, too.

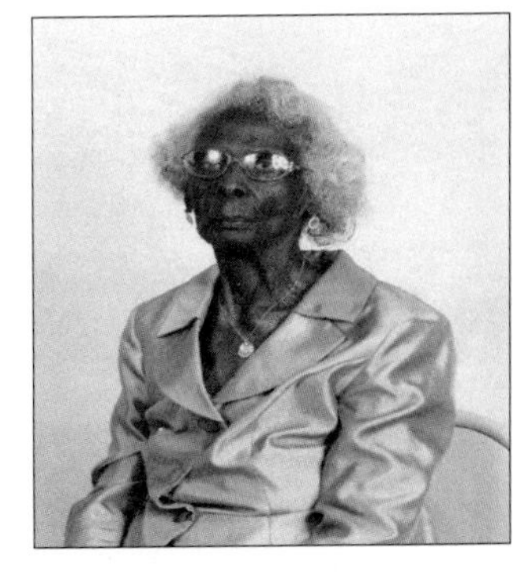

Onethia Elliott was born on Sandy Island in 1914, the daughter of Hammond and Sarah Washington and great-great-granddaughter of founder Phillip Washington.

Her brother Prince's boat gently knocks against the dock as he waits there to ferry Onethia and other islanders across the river to work. Many of the men are plasterers and work on the mainland in Conway. Prince's calloused hands pull the oars through the currents of the Waccamaw, flicking river mist onto their faces. It takes just under an hour to make the trip to Brookgreen, and Onethia thanks God for a safe journey. When she returns in the evening, she will be sweaty from the hard work, longing for a hot meal, grateful to be home.

Like her parents before her, she built a life on the island with fellow islander John, and together they raised seven children in a home at the top of Mount Arena. Like other residents, they worked hard to provide for themselves and their children. In the 1930s when rice production on the

Onethia Elliott's residence.

island came mostly to a halt, they looked to the outside world for work. To support her family, Onethia worked in the homes of wealthy white families in Myrtle Beach for more than 60 years.

In a rowboat, the act of returning was a labor in itself. Each afternoon, Elliott came home to the welcoming laughs and cries of her children. But her day did not end there. She still had to prepare dinner before rest. Keeping two families, her white family and her own, fed was no small feat, especially because her home didn't have electricity. For over 50 years, Elliott did the extra chores required in a home without power. She would haul wood from the oxen cart, fill the chimney with wood, stoke the fire, wait and wait, and then prepare the dinner for herself and her family.

Yvonne Tucker-Harris, who grew up on the island, remembers the nights of her childhood in kerosene glow, hurrying to complete chores and homework before it got too dark. "Living by lamplight, we didn't have sufficient lighting to read all the time, so that restricted my desire to read a lot," she said. "When it got dark, we had a lamp in the family room area, Momma had a lamp in their bedroom, and there was a lamp near where the kitchen was. But that was it! If we were going to different rooms, we had to take a flashlight or a lamp with us. Because you didn't put a kerosene lamp in every room and leave it lit." In the mornings, Harris would go to the schoolhouse on the island, hurrying to their teacher's calling, while her grandfather would row across the river to work as a bricklayer in Georgetown.

One day in 1960, her uncle, Franklin Tucker, crossed the Waccamaw River in a low-riding motorboat and then drove to Georgetown to pick up his brother Albert's bags from the bus station. Half on a whim, Tucker decided to take the U.S. Air Force test, like his brother, who had just come home. He was 20 years old and willing; it was a moment for change. When he arrived, the Air Force recruiter was out of the office, so Tucker went next door to take the Naval exam instead. The next day, he was on his way to Columbia to receive a physical examination and to begin bootcamp. From there, Tucker traveled to Great Lakes, Illinois and to Long Beach, California where he boarded a ship. But he left Sandy Island, like many of the young men and women in his community, like Onethia each morning, knowing, hoping he would return.

In 1964, Tucker came home. "Nothing much had changed," Tucker said. "But they were getting electricity over there." Island homes now had indoor bathrooms,

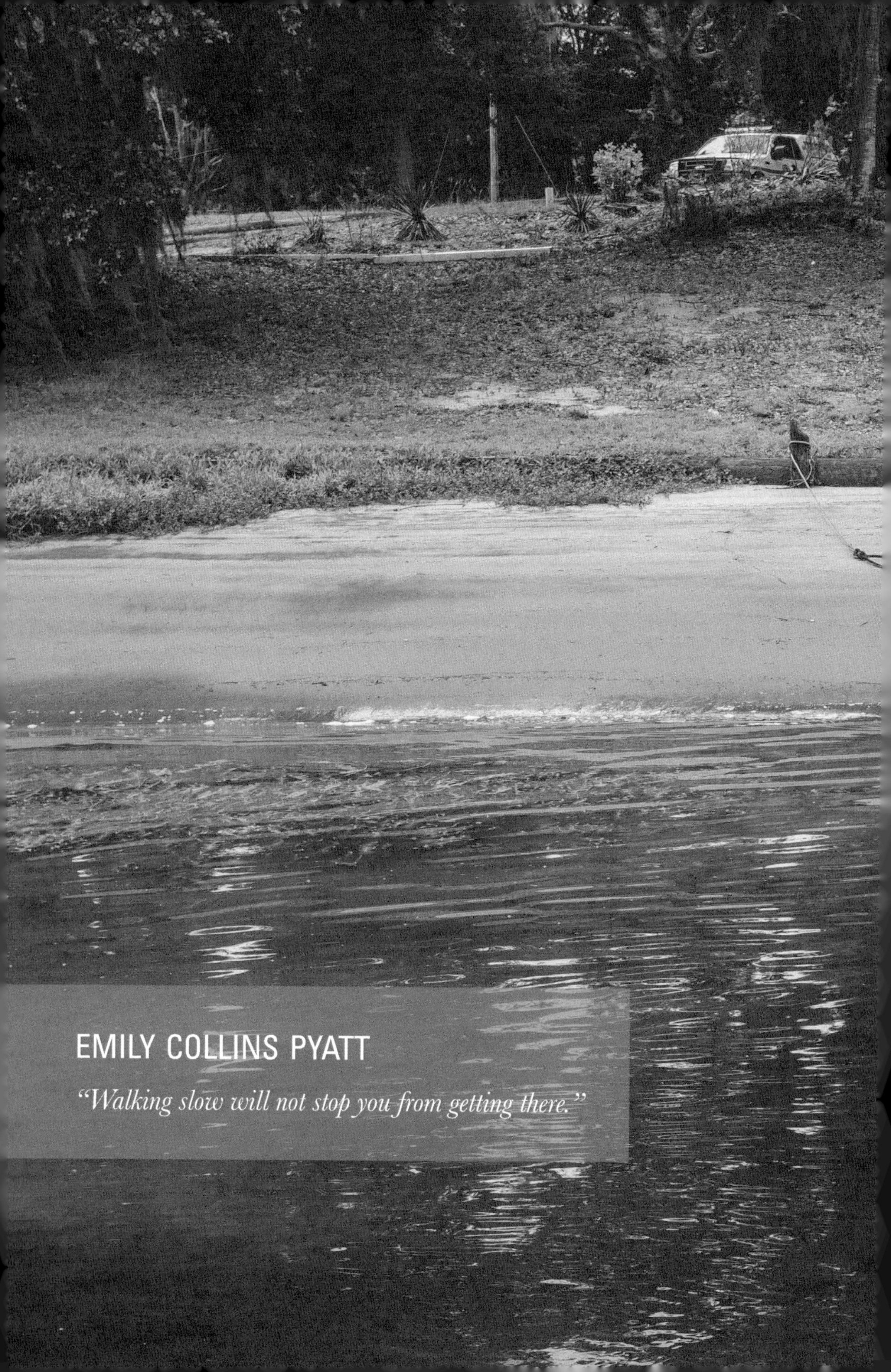

EMILY COLLINS PYATT

"Walking slow will not stop you from getting there."

YAMAHA

Yvonne Tucker-Harris, retired Army Colonel.

electric stoves, refrigerators and freezers—all the conveniences of the mainland. Before, islanders relied on keeping meat and milk cool in iceboxes or deep wells. Tucker remembers traveling off the island to buy ice for home. "You'd buy 50 pounds and have 25 pounds when you got home," he said, recalling hot summers on the Waccamaw neck.

The push to bring utilities to the island began in the 1950s under the leadership of Phillip Washington's great-great-grandson, Prince. Born on the island, Washington traveled in his youth, working in factories in New York and sailing the Atlantic as a merchant seaman. He returned home when his parents needed him. On the island, he had many roles: shad fisherman, ferryman, and deacon at New Bethel Church. Washington acted out the duties of his deaconship, and in the footsteps of his grandfather, became the island's leader from the 1950s until his death in 1975.

For a decade, Washington worked tirelessly on his greatest project: bringing electricity to Sandy Island. He commuted across the Waccamaw and then onward to Columbia to speak directly with South Carolina Governor James F. Byrnes. It was with the enlistment of Senator C.C. Grimes Jr., who formally requested the directors of the Santee Cooper Public Service Authority to provide the island with electricity, that the islanders' hope for electricity was finally realized. The state ran the submarine lines across the river and cut through five miles of forest thicket to lay the power lines across the island. A little under a decade later, in 1972, Washington ensured the installation of telephone service on the island. Power on the island gave increased comfort and security on the island and connections to the outside world across the water. When Washington first flipped the ceremonial switch which turned the lights on at Sandy Island, he said, "Electricity won't bring new life, but it will renew life."

Yvonne Tucker-Harris, who studied by the dim light of the kerosene lamp, remembers that her studying improved dramatically once electricity came to the island. She could study at night, especially in the winter, when it got dark around 4:30. "It was so much easier," she said. "We had light. You could just flip on a light and read." The children of the island had to overcome one less hurdle to excel in school, something so valued on the island. But even electricity wasn't enough to stop the exodus off the island. Even as Washington fought for the implementation of modern conveniences to renew and renew again life on Sandy Island, men and women crossed the Waccamaw for work, school, and duty, then stayed. Now, islanders are scattered across the country, but Sandy Island still calls its children home.

LOW TIDE ON THE ISLAND

Laura Herriott still remembers the two-room Sandy Island School. The island was known for its spelling bee champions, who won repeatedly at the county and state level. Teachers would stand students outside, near the two outbuildings about fifty feet away from the back of the building, and call out words to them, making sure they projected their voices. The school house didn't have a lot of educational materials, but there was an encyclopedia set and used textbooks from a white school on the mainland. It was enough, and those children in the classroom would go on to complete high school and college at a much higher rate than African Americans in the rest of Georgetown county.

After finishing sixth grade, Herriott would climb into the diesel-powered school boat and chug across the river to where a bus was waiting for her and the other children to take them on to Howard High School. Sandy Islanders stuck together. They ate lunch together. They played together. They would board that slow boat across the river home. But soon, some islanders would take a different path.

In 1963, 80 miles to the south of Sandy Island, a Black, 15-year-old girl named Millicent Brown walked through the doors to Charleston's all-white Rivers High School and desegregated South Carolina under the then-nine-year-old Supreme Court ruling that racially segregated schools were inherently unequal. Just as Brown met her new teacher, the intercom announced a fire drill. The entire school emptied in single-file lines in response to a phoned-in bomb threat, the first of three that day.

The violent climate surrounding the desegregation of public schools prevented many Black parents from moving their children into white schools, a choice they had under "freedom of choice." Because they feared retribution at their work or neighborhood, Black schools stayed Black and white schools stayed white. In 1966, South Carolina increased its desegregation efforts by closing smaller schools with what it termed as "inadequate facilities" that were used exclusively by one race, usually honing in on rural, Black schools. The schoolhouse on Sandy Island was one of those schools. Elementary students would join their older friends on the

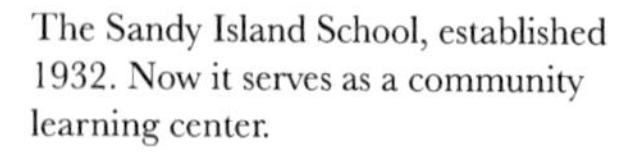
The Sandy Island School, established 1932. Now it serves as a community learning center.

trek across the river. Suddenly, the bus was not a special ride reserved only for middle and high-school children.

But it would be another 15 years before full integration would come to Georgetown. In 1981, after a contentious November school board meeting over questions as to why there were two high schools in such an underpopulated county, three men took gasoline to the mostly-white Winyah High School, and burned it nearly down, reportedly to avoid combining Howard High School, the African American school, and Winyah, the mostly white school. Winyah had been open to Black students since the school closures of 1966, but only a few Sandy Islanders, including Yvonne Harris Tucker, had elected to go to Winyah. While Howard was considered a vocational high school, Winyah, some islanders believed, was the ticket to college. Tucker stayed at Winyah for two years, but left because "the white teachers were not as helpful to African American students." Tucker graduated from Howard in 1974, finished college and graduate school, and went on to become a Colonel in the Army.

Before the consolidations, Sandy Island parents could choose to send their students across the Waccamaw for their primary education or remain at the island school. When the state closed their school, the island's legacy of educating its own children, many who academically excelled beyond their peers across the county, ended.

In the years after Sandy Island School closed, the trek across the tannin-dyed Waccamaw seemed to widen as more men and women left their island home for war or work, and families moved across the water to be closer

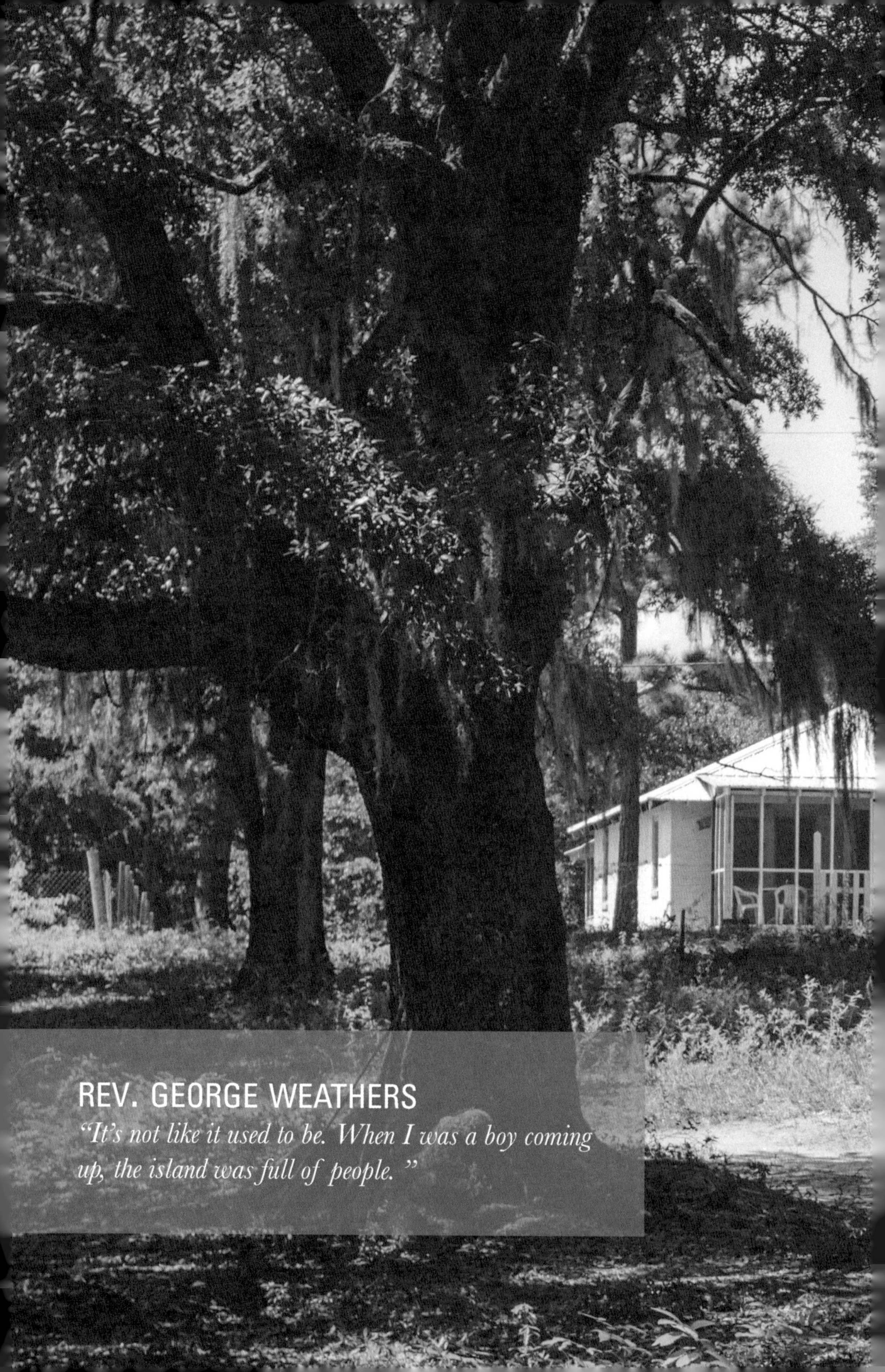

REV. GEORGE WEATHERS

"It's not like it used to be. When I was a boy coming up, the island was full of people."

COTTAGE

Reverend George Weathers.

to schools. By the early 1990s, what had once been a community of more than 300 members had dwindled to only 135 permanent residents.

In 1992, this island was threatened further when two men from the mainland approached the community with plans to build a bridge. Roger Milliken, a textile magnate from the upstate, and E. Craig Wall, a wealthy timberman, presented the bridge as a way to transport timber which they would harvest from the northern, uninhabited region on the island. Together, the two men owned 9,000 acres—the lion's share of the island's total 12,000. What Milliken and Walls concealed from the community was that after they harvested the timber, they planned to develop that land into a gated golfing resort.

"When I first heard they were going to build a bridge, I thought it was a good idea," Reverend George Weathers said. But Weathers and the community got word of the development plans that Milliken and Walls had submitted for approval, and they learned that residents of the island wouldn't be able to drive over the bridge—except in an ambulance or hearse.

Islanders enlisted their own legal representation through the Southern Environmental Law center in Chapel Hill, NC, and sought the advice of other African American island communities in South Carolina that had been developed, including Saint Helena Island and Hilton Head. "After going around and viewing the areas where people of color lived before development—it's not there anymore," said

Beulah Pyatt, a resident of the island and owner of the general store. High-rise hotels and golf courses increased property values and property taxes so quickly that the local communities—the Gullah Geechee communities that had lived there for generations—couldn't afford to keep their houses or property.

Local environmentalists within the South Carolina Coastal Conservation League also argued against the proposed bridge on Sandy Island. However, the state initially appeared to side with Wall and Milliken. The State Historic Office surveyed the community in 1996, as part of the legal battle, and released a report stating, "Sandy Island has no distinct culture [to preserve]." The islanders and conservationist then had to focus solely on the island's wetlands, swamps, and the red-cockaded woodpecker that made its home among the towering longleaf pines. In 1996, after a four-year legal battle, the South Carolina Department of Transportation purchased Milliken and Walls' landholdings on Sandy Island for about $10 million with $1 million contributed by the national Nature Conservancy. In 2011, the South Carolina Department of Transportation relinquished the land on Sandy Island to the Nature Conservancy.

Today, the task of preserving Sandy Island is twofold. Beyond the need for further improvement to the island's infrastructure, fewer than 40 people currently live on the island. Most of the islanders are elderly, and too many voices are lost each year.

Charles Pyatt, Retired Army Sargent First Class.

"I would love to see people come back home and make Sandy Island what it used to be," said Charles Pyatt, head of the island's voluntary fire department. Pyatt always viewed Sandy Island as his home, even after 24 years in the Army. Currently, his brother, Issac Pyatt, Georgetown County chief magistrate, is building a home back on the island.

Yet there is no easy solution to stop the population decline. In 2015, after almost 20 years of campaigning by Pyatt and other members of the community, the island received a brand new school boat from the South Carolina State Department of Education. Though the vessel, christened the *New Prince Washington*, was a much needed improvement, there are only seven students for it to transport. The school boat mainly functions as an accessible ferry for the entire island community. It provides the first regular and public transportation to and from the island.

Despite recent improvements to transportation, crossing the river is still deemed difficult. "Only thing I can think of to attract people back is a bridge," said Laura Herriott, owner of Wilma's Cottage, a bed and breakfast on the island. A bridge on the community's terms could benefit current residents, especially the elders who now struggle with the physical demands of crossing the Waccamaw—walking through sandy terrain and across floating docks and then climbing into cars parked on both sides of the river.

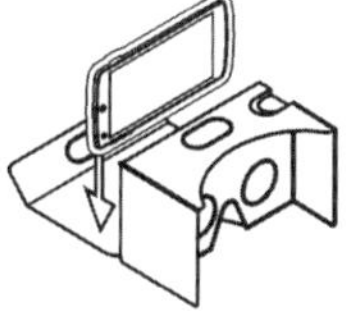

See the homes that Charles Pyatt and other islanders are building by visiting ccu.press/vr.

But a bridge might not be enough to bring people back to the island. Land protected by the Nature Conservancy is not available for development, and few available lots remain on the residential side. People who moved away from Sandy Island, either by losing land or by choice, must wait for property to become available and then purchase land directly from an owner.

At this low tide, Sandy Island's future remains uncertain. In response to the dwindling population, the community is focusing on preserving the history and identity of the island and its importance to the Waccamaw Neck. Community members now operate a tour service, general store, and two bed and breakfasts to attract tourists to learn and experience the island's natural and historic resources—"It was like God had it planned for me to actually get into business," said Rommy Pyatt, owner and operator of Tours de Sandy Island. Though Pyatt lives 70 miles to the south in Charleston, he's grateful for his childhood on Sandy Island that has led him into business operating his tour service. On his tours, he teaches visitors about the history and culture of the island. After hearing the old school boat that carried countless children and residents, including himself, across the Waccamaw, would be up for auction, he seized the opportunity and purchased it.

Sandy Island has been protected from development, a rarity along the southern coast.

Now, visitors board the repainted and refurbished old *Prince Washington* to the island. Crossing the river, Pyatt speaks above the rumble of the engine as he points to the rice paddies along the way. He jokingly encourages visitors to take pockets of sand back to the mainland. Once docked, he shows his customers into the general store, where his mother, Beulah, greets them. Within walking distance is

CHARLES PYATT

"It's a short trip to go to the mainland. Years ago, it took 15 minutes or more. Now, it takes five or ten."

60

Wilma's Cottage, where visitors briefly experience island culture through her Gullah Geechee cooking and hospitality in what was once her grandparents' home.

From across the river, Sandy Island looks like a small community. But these businesses represent the strength and value that has always lived on the island. "It took me going away from the island to be able to turn around and look at it and see the opportunities," Pyatt says. "Sometimes you're in one place all your life, and you really can't see what's right there because of that one tree blocking you from seeing the whole forest."

STILL STANDING

In the morning, before the sun has risen, seven children make their way to the dock. Their life vests are tightly secured across their chests. They board the boat, glance back at the shoreline, imagining the island children who have come before them. Back then, boys played freely in the river and splashed one another. The girls, warned never to go into the water, stood off to the side in the grass playing games.

All children seated aboard, the *New Prince Washington* school boat slowly pushes away from the dock. Every weekday, children take the 10-minute trip across the river, similar to those who preceded them. Their only option to get to school is to cross the wide water.

In 1964, 30 students made this crossing. Prince Washington pulled up in a pale blue school boat and the first group of children found a space to sit. With barely enough room to wiggle, they sat shoulder to shoulder. Washington dropped off the first group of children and headed back for the second round.

Today the boat's new name beams across the Waccamaw. In red and yellow lettering, the children see *New Prince*

Washington and "South Carolina Public Schools" reflected, in pieces, in the tide. This is the only public school boat in South Carolina. After many years of lobbying by the islanders and local activists, Georgetown County finally agreed to replace the outdated and unsafe former boat. They load onto the glossy white vessel with plenty of room to spread out. As the boat moves through the water, the children look out at the familiar banks. In the middle of the Waccamaw, the water stretches further and, for a moment, appears still. Like their parents and others before them, they have always traveled by boat. They have always known the river. When the boat arrives at the mainland, they board the school bus, full of other children.

Children on the landing at Sandy Island, circa 1930s (unidentified) and 2017 (Treyevon Williams and Mekhi Robinson). Historic image courtesy of Brookgreen Gardens.

With the demands of school and work, living off the island is more convenient. Whether by choice or circumstance, many Sandy Islanders have moved away from the island. Without having to cross the river, parents walk only a few steps to their cars for work and children wait near their homes to board the school bus for school. But the few residents who have stayed on the island are committed to the river and the land. They accept the added steps of crossing the river to access their cars, mail, the school bus, and even discard of trash. It was a bargain made long ago. They stand in the same place as their ancestors and hold on to the island's legacy. Yet those who have moved to the mainland remember that same legacy and hold it close.

Martha Cousey, daughter of Sandy Island residents.

Martha Cousey lives in Conway, South Carolina, but is still part of the Sandy Island community. Her parents, George and Helen Lance, were once residents on Sandy Island. "It's always been a family. We are scattered all over the US and foreign countries. And when something happens we all come together from all over. It's still home. It's still family. We all have that love and that closeness."

New Bethel Missionary Baptist Church brings many home each month. Each Sunday, New Bethel's burgundy and silver pontoon picks up current pastor Karon Jackson, deacons, and families from the mainland for church service. Coming from their homes in Myrtle Beach, Pawleys Island, Conway, or Georgetown, dressed in their Sunday best, these families wait diligently every Sunday at the mainland's dock for the boat to arrive. Once aboard and on their way, the river's current echoes the names of some those who have drowned since 1955: Robert Elliott, Johnny Collins, Madelyn Nelson, Connie Nelson, Prince Washington, Alice H. Collins, Geneva Singleton Herriott, Sheila Herriott, Eva Herriott, Bentlee Herriott, James Herriott, James Johnson Jr., Willie Deas, Lou Ann Robinson, Rishard Pyatt, Shaquatia Robinson, and many more.

Parents check again and again to secure their children's life jackets. Looking out to the water, they study the river and understand its language. The direction of the current, how the water splashes against the boat, how the waves dip or lie flat. The river once served as a means of freedom and opportunity; the river brought safety. After slavery, it continued to shelter the people from the racism that still persisted, but afforded them more opportunities. Descendants purchased land, created institutions such as school and church, and governed themselves in relative peace. But that freedom came at a price. The Waccamaw took valuable lives. From this, Sandy Islanders learned to approach the river with caution and grace. Although thankful for what the river offers, they are respectful of its power.

The first *Prince Washington* school boat. When decommissioned in 2016, Rommy Pyatt bought it at auction, and refurbished it to run tours on the island.

Approaching Sandy Island, people catch sight of the red and green rooftops of Beulah and Sam Pyatt's general store and Charles Pyatt's home. When the pontoon docks, they walk up the ramp, holding on to the silver railings. A bus carries them along the sandy, unpaved road a mile inland. Along the way, they pass by the school—now a community center—and small groups of homes. The bus passes over small hills before pulling in front of the ivory building. A quaint sign reads "New Bethel Baptist Church" with two small crosses on each side.

The *New Prince Washington*, the new school boat won after a long campaign in 2016. The boat now serves as an accessible ferry, with regular service for all island residents.

Entering the church, people sit in rows of red-felted pews. The stained-glass windows cast a transparent blue light across the room. Resting just above the windowsill, on each window, the hand-painted lettering reads "In Memory Of" followed by the names of descendants: Pyatt, Washington, Herriott, Tucker, Lance, Nelson, Robinson, Collins. These names, these hands, built the community. And hold it up.

In service, people clap, sing along with the choir, and bow their heads as a deacon leads prayer. They listen intently to the pastor as he speaks and respond with "amen" and "preach!" In these moments, as everyone comes together under one roof, it feels like old times. When two churches were active on the island, there were enough people to fill both buildings. Now, fewer than 40 people live on Sandy Island full time and most of the community is elderly. "The island was full of homes, it was full of people, and now it's just almost a small token," Cousey says. And there are elders living off the island who desire to return to spend the time they have left back home.

Where will Sandy Island go from here? Some believe that the rapid development of the surrounding Grand Strand will eventually cross over and envelop the island. Others hope that this African American community will continue to maintain its culture and unique way of life. Having shared their voices and the history of their ancestors in this book, we hope you can look at Sandy Island's story and see its triumphs. This self-reliant community survived against all odds and made a permanent imprint in South Carolina's history. We hope you recognize the importance of this community before its conclusion. There are fewer and fewer people on the island each year. The voices are truly at low tide.

Those who are still rooted to the island, and even those living off the island, look to the children. They pass down the trades of hard work and leadership from one generation to the next. Just across the river, on the mainland, children wake up before the sun and wait at the bus stop. On the island, those seven children, waking up before sun, walking to the river. Even though the future of Sandy Island is unclear, Sandy Islanders find hope within the children. Whether on the island or beyond it, the culture and identity of Sandy Island will live on.

XAVIER TUCKER

"I live with my grandma and my sister. My grandad drives the school boat. And my grandma, my sister, and I come up and pick up the other kids, and we go to the school boat. Get on the school boat and go across, and get on the bus."

BIBLIOGRAPHY

Allston, Robert F. W., and J. H. Easterby. *The South Carolina Rice Plantation As Revealed in the Papers of Robert F.W. Allston*. Columbia, S.C.: University of South Carolina Press, 2004.

Beall, Kyle. "A Study of Environmental Politics: The Sandy Island Fiasco." *The South Carolina Environmental Law Journal* 6 (Summer 1997): 17-41.

Chandler, Genevieve W. *Coming Through: Voices of a South Carolina Gullah Community from WPA Oral Histories*. Columbia, S.C: Univ. of South Carolina Press, 2008.

Dusinberre, William. *Them Dark Days: Slavery in the American Rice Swamps*. Athens, GA: University of Georgia Press, 2006.

"Families speak after tragic boat accident." Live5News. 2009. http://www.live5news.com/story/9869336/families-speak-after-tragic-boat-accident.

Hurley, Suzanne Cameron Linder, Marta Leslie Thacker, and Agnes Leland Baldwin. *Historical Atlas of the Rice Plantations of Georgetown County and the Santee River*. Columbia, S.C.: Published by the South Carolina Dept. of Archives and History for the Historic Ricefields Association, 2001.

Joyner, Charles W. *Down by the Riverside: A South Carolina Slave Community*. Urbana: University of Illinois Press, 1985.

Khan, Aisha. "Residents mark one year anniversary of Sandy Island boat tragedy." SCNow. December 31, 2012. http://www.scnow.com/news/local/article_61ce2d6e-4697-5fea-9a42-4e6bd1ea15dd.html

Kouri, Christopher. "When a Man Starts Out to Build a World: The History of Sandy island." Penn Center Sea Island Preservation Project. St. Helena Island, South Carolina, 1994.

National Park Service. *Low Country Gullah Culture Special Resource Study and Final Environmental Impact Statement*. Atlanta, GA: NPS Southeast Regional Office, 2005. 27, 35-37.

Nichols, Patricia Causey. "Linguistic Change in Gullah: Sex, Age, and Mobility." PhD diss., Stanford University, 1976.

Pringle, Elizabeth W. Allston. *Chronicles of Chicora Wood*. New York: C. Scribner's Sons, 1922.

Pyatt, Thomas. *The Gullah People of Sandy Island: A Tribute to the Gullah People of Sandy Island*, S.C. Copyright T.J. Pyatt, 2005.

Rogers, George C. *The History of Georgetown County, South Carolina*. Spartanburg, S.C.: Published for the Georgetown County Historical Society [by] the Reprint Co, 1995.

SCNow Staff. "Third body found after Sandy Island boating accident." SCNow. February 20, 2009. http://www.scnow.com/news/local/article_ab49a36e-39d2-58cc-bd83-db358a02c889.html.

Stephens, Dean. "A miracle child and a push for a new ferry." ABCNews4. June 2, 2011. http://abcnews4.com/archive/a-miracle-child-and-the-push-for-a-new-ferry.

FACES OF THE PROJECT

PRODUCTION TEAM

Quinten Ameris, *Writer/Researcher*
Kaitlyn Cegielski, *Designer*
Shonte Clement, *Writer/Researcher*
Skylar Delaney, *Illustrator*
Brooks Leibee, *Videographer*
Jesse Lindler, *Packaging Designer*
Maggie Nichols, *Graduate Writer/Researcher*
Jose Rangel, *Researcher*
DeAndrae Preston, *Musician/Composer*
Alexa Stress, *Packaging Designer*
Ronda Taylor, *Graduate Writer/Researcher*
Madia Walker, *Website Design*
Angelis Washington, *Community Historian Advisor*
Haley Yarborough, *Photographer*

COMMUNITY REVIEWERS

Martha Cousey
Beulah Pyatt
Carolyn Pyatt
Charles Pyatt
Yvonne Tucker-Harris

FACULTY ADVISORS

Eric Crawford, *Assistant Professor of Music*
Alli Crandell, *Project Manager, The Athenaeum Press, and Director of Digital Initiatives*
Scott Mann, *Production Manager, The Athenaeum Press, and Associate Professor of Visual Arts*
Trisha O'Connor, *Director, The Athenaeum Press and Media Executive-in-Residence*

FACES OF THE PRESS

DAN ENNIS

Dean, Thomas W. and Robin W. Edwards College of Humanities and Fine Arts

ATHENAEUM PRESS EXECUTIVE COMMITTEE

Doug Bell, *University Communications*

Pamela Martin, *Politics*

Maggi Morehouse, *History*

Keaghan Turner, *English*

ACKNOWLEDGMENTS

Historic images are the courtesy of the Georgetown Digital Public Library, Brookgreen Gardens, and the Pawleys Island Civic Society. All other images are original to this project.

We would like to thank the Sandy Island community, both on and off the island, for offering their time and stories to our project. We'd like to especially thank Martha Cousey, Onethia Elliott, Rosalyn Geathers, Yvonne Tucker-Harris, Ashanti Herriott, Laura Herriott, Braylen Nesmith, L.W. Paul, Beulah Pyatt, Charles Pyatt, Emily Collins Pyatt, Rommy Pyatt, Trenton Pyatt, Mackhi Robinson, Franklin Tucker, Xavier Tucker, and Rev. and Mrs. George Weathers.

We have had the pleasure of collaborating with them for the last two years to tell this story. We look forward to continuing to build on this project with familiar and new faces in the years to come.

To follow this project and view the additional video content, visit ccu.press/lowtide.

Made in the USA
Columbia, SC
18 January 2021